I0147253

Toyokichi Iyenaga

The Constitutional Development of Japan, 1853-1881

Toyokichi Iyenaga

The Constitutional Development of Japan, 1853-1881

ISBN/EAN: 9783337165628

Printed in Europe, USA, Canada, Australia, Japan

Cover: Foto ©ninafisch / pixelio.de

More available books at **www.hansebooks.com**

JOHNS HOPKINS UNIVERSITY STUDIES

IN

HISTORICAL AND POLITICAL SCIENCE

HERBERT B. ADAMS, Editor

History is past Politics and Politics present History.—*Freeman*

NINTH SERIES

IX

THE CONSTITUTIONAL DEVELOPMENT OF JAPAN.   1853–1881

By TOYOKICHI IYENAGA, PH. D.

Professor of Political Science in Tokio Senmon-Gakko

BALTIMORE

THE JOHNS HOPKINS PRESS

PUBLISHED MONTHLY

September, 1891

COPYRIGHT, 1891, BY N. MURRAY.

ISAAC FRIEDENWALD CO., PRINTERS,
BALTIMORE.

CONTENTS.

THE CONSTITUTIONAL DEVELOPMENT OF JAPAN. 1853—1881.

INTRODUCTORY.

The power which destroyed Japanese feudalism and changed in that country an absolute into a constitutional monarchy was a resultant of manifold forces. The most apparent of these forces is the foreign influence. Forces less visible but more potent, tending in this direction, are those influences resulting from the growth of commerce and trade, from the diffusion of western science and knowledge among the people, and from the changes in social habits and religious beliefs. The truth of the solidarity of the varied interests of a social organism is nowhere so well exemplified as in the history of modern Japan. Her remarkable political development would have been impossible had there been no corresponding social, educational, religious, economic and industrial changes. In order to trace the constitutional development of New Japan, it is therefore necessary :

1. To ascertain the political condition of the country at and after the advent of foreigners in 1853.

2. To describe the form of government of the Restoration.

3. To examine the state of commerce, industry, education and social life of Japan at each stage of her political transformations.

4. To recount the constitutional changes from the Restoration to the Promulgation of the New. Constitution.

As a novice in travel marks the broad outlines, the general features and more important products of the country he visits for the first time, so I shall dwell upon the historic landmarks of Japanese constitutional development. This development no writer, native or foreign, has yet attempted to trace. I shall withstand as much as possible the temptation to refer to the multitude of events which are more or less associated with the constitutional movement. I shall endeavor to ascertain from the edicts, decrees, and proclamations of the Emperor, from the orders and manifestos of the Shogun, from the native authors and journals, from the memorials and correspondence of prominent men, both native and foreign, the trend of our constitutional development. I shall also endeavor to note the leading ideas and principles which, after manifesting themselves in various forms, have at last crystallized into the New Constitution of Japan.

CHAPTER I.

Beginning of the Constitutional Movement.

The constitutional movement of Japan began in a spontaneous agitation of the whole body politic when the nation was irritated by the sudden contact with foreigners. The sense of national weakness added a force to this agitation. Had not the foreigners come, the Restoration might have been effected, feudalism might have been abolished, but the new Japanese constitution would hardly have seen the day. Had the government of Japan at the time of the advent of foreigners been in the strong hand of a Taiko or an Iyeyasu, the rulers might have been greatly exercised by the extraordinary event, but public opinion for reform would hardly have been called forth, and the birth of constitutional liberty would long have been delayed. As the vicés of King John and the indifference and ignorance of the first two Georges of England begat the strength and hope of the English Parliament, so the public opinion of Japan sprouted out of the ruins of the Shogunate régime. We must therefore seek for the beginning of the Constitutional Movement of Japan in the peculiar circumstances in which she found herself between 1853 and 1868.

The advent of Commodore Perry in 1853 was to Japan like the intrusion of a foreign queen into a beehive. The country was stirred to its depth. Let us note what a native chronicler[1] says about the condition of Japan at the arrival of Perry:

"It was in the summer of 1853 that an individual named Perry, who called himself the envoy of the United States of

---

[1] Genje Yume Monogatari. Translated by Mr. Ernest Satow, and published in the columns of the *Japan Mail.*

America, suddenly arrived at Uraga, in the Province of Sagami, with four ships of war, declaring that he brought a letter from his country to Japan and that he wished to deliver it to the sovereign. The governor of the place, Toda Idzu No Kami, much alarmed by this extraordinary event, hastened to the spot to inform himself of its meaning. The envoy stated, in reply to questions, that he desired to see a chief minister in order to explain the object of his visit and to hand over to him the letter with which he was charged. The governor then despatched a messenger on horseback with all haste to carry this information to the castle of Yedo, where a great scene of confusion ensued on his arrival. Fresh messengers followed, and the Shogun Iyeyoshi, on receiving them, was exceedingly troubled, and summoned all the officials[1] to a council. At first the affair seemed so sudden and so formidable that they were too alarmed to open their mouths, but in the end orders were issued to the great clans to keep strict watch at various points on the shore, as it was possible that the 'barbarian' vessels might proceed to commit acts of violence.   Presently a learned Chinese scholar was sent to Uraga, had an interview with the American envoy, and returned with the letter, which expressed the desire of the United States to establish friendship and inter-course with Japan, and said, according to this account, that if they met with a refusal they should commence hostilities. Thereupon the Shogun was greatly distressed, and again summoned a council. He also asked the opinion of the Daimios. The assembled officials were exceedingly dis-turbed, and nearly broke their hearts over consultations which lasted all day and all night. The nobles and retired nobles in Yedo were informed that they were at liberty to state any ideas they might have on the subject, and, although they all gave their opinions, the diversity of propositions was so great that no decision was arrived at. The military class had, during a long peace, neglected military arts ; they

---

[1] The original gives names of some prominent officials thus summoned.

had given themselves up to pleasure and luxury, and there were very few who had put on armor for many years, so that they were greatly alarmed at the prospect that war might break out at a moment's notice, and began to run hither and thither in search of arms. The city of Yedo and the surrounding villages were in a great tumult. And there was such a state of confusion among all classes that the governors of the city were compelled to issue a notification to the people, and this in the end had the effect of quieting the general anxiety. But in the castle never was a decision further from being arrived at, and, whilst time was being thus idly wasted, the envoy was constantly demanding an answer. So at last they decided that it would be best to arrange the affair quietly, to give the foreigners the articles they wanted, and to put off sending an answer to the letter— to tell the envoy that in an affair of such importance to the state no decision could be arrived at without mature consideration, and that he had better go away; that in a short time he should get a definite answer. The envoy agreed, and after sending a message, to say that he should return in the following spring for his answer, set sail from Uraga with his four ships."[1]

Thus was the renowned commander kept away for awhile. He went, however, of his own accord. Perry was an astute diplomatist. He knew that time was needed for the impressions which he and his magnificent fleet had made upon the country to produce their natural effect.

The news of Perry's visit and demands spread far and wide with remarkable rapidity. The government and the people were deeply stirred. Soon the song of the " red-bearded barbarians " and of the black ships was in everybody's mouth. The question " What shall Japan do when the barbarians come next spring?" became the absorbing theme of the day.

---

[1] This is also quoted in F. O. Adams's History of Japan, Vol. I., p. 109. I have compared the passage with the original and quote here with some modifications in the translation.

There was now but one of two policies which Japan could pursue, either to shut up the country or to admit the foreigners' demand. There was no middle course left. The American envoy would no longer listen to the dilatory policy with which the Japanese had just bought a few months' respite from anxiety.

The majority of the ruling class, the Samurai, were in favor of the exclusion policy. So was the court of Kioto. But the views of the court of Yedo were different. The court of Yedo had many men of intelligence, common sense and experience—men who had seen the American envoy and his squadron, equipped with all the contrivances for killing men and devastating the country. These men knew too well that resistance to the foreigners was futile and perilous.

Thus was the country early divided into two clearly defined parties, the Jo-i[1] party and the Kai-Koku party.

Meanwhile, the autumn and winter of 1853 passed. The spring of 1854 soon came, and with it the intractable " barbarians." Let us hear the author of Genje Yume Monogatari relate the return of Perry and the great discussion that ensued at the court of Yedo :

" Early in 1854 Commodore Perry returned, and the question of acceding to his demands was again hotly debated. The old prince of Mito was opposed to it, and contended that the admission of foreigners into Japan would ruin it. 'At first,' said he, 'they will give us philosophical instruments, machinery and other curiosities; will take ignorant people in, and, trade being their chief object, they will manage bit by bit to impoverish the country, after which they will treat us just as they like—perhaps behave with the greatest rudeness and insult us, and end by swallowing up Japan. If we do not drive them away now we shall never have another opportunity. If we now resort to a dilatory method of proceeding we shall regret it afterwards when it will be of no use.'

---

[1] Jo-i means to expel the barbarians; Kai-Koku means to open the country.

" The officials (of the Shogun), however, argued otherwise and said : 'If we try to drive them away they will immediately commence hostilities, and then we shall be obliged to fight. If we once get into a dispute we shall have an enemy to fight who will not be easily disposed of. He does not care how long a time he must spend over it, but he will come with myriads of men-of-war and surround our shores completely ; he will capture our junks and blockade our ports, and deprive us of all hope of protecting our coasts. However large a number of ships we might destroy, he is so — accustomed to that sort of thing that he would not care in the least. Even supposing that our troops were animated by patriotic zeal in the commencement of the war, after they had been fighting for several years their patriotic zeal would naturally become relaxed, the soldiers would become fatigued, and for this we should have to thank ourselves. Soldiers who have distinguished themselves are rewarded by grants of land, or else you attack and seize the enemy's territory and that becomes your own property ; so every man is encouraged to fight his best. But in a war with foreign countries a man may undergo hardships for years, may fight as if his life were worth nothing, and, as all the land in this country already has owners, there will be none to be given away as rewards ; so we shall have to give rewards in words or money. In time the country would be put to an immense expense and the people be plunged into misery. Rather than allow this, as we are not the equals of foreigners in the mechanical arts, let us have intercourse with foreign countries, learn their drill and tactics, and when we have made the nation as united as one family, we shall be able to go abroad and give lands in foreign countries to those who have distinguished themselves in battle. The soldiers will vie with one another in displaying their intrepidity, and it will not be too late then to declare war. Now we shall have to defend ourselves against these foreign enemies, skilled in the use of mechanical appliances, with our soldiers whose military skill has considerably diminished during a long peace of three hundred years, and we certainly could not feel sure of victory, especially in a naval war.' "[1]

The Kai-Koku party, the party in favor of opening the country, triumphed, and the treaty was finally concluded between the United States and Japan on the 31st of March, 1854. After the return of Commodore Perry to America, Townsend Harris was sent by the United States Government as Consul-General to Japan. He negotiated the commercial treaty between the United States and Japan on July 29, 1858.

At the heels of the Americans followed the English, French, Russians, Dutch, and other nations. Japan's foreign relations became more and more complicated and therefore difficult to manage.

The discussion quoted above is a type of the arguments used by the Jo-i party and the Kai-Koku party. The history of Japanese politics from 1853 to 1868 is the history of the struggle between these two parties, each of which soon changed its name. As the Jo-i party allied itself with the court of Kioto, it became the O-sei or Restoration party. As the Kai-Koku party was associated with the court of Shogun, it became the Bakufu party. The struggle ended in the triumph of the Restoration party. But by that time the Jo-i party, from a cause which I shall soon mention, had been completely transformed and converted to the Western ideas.

Among the leaders of the Jo-i party was Nariaki, the old prince of Mito. He belonged to one of the San Kay (three families), out of which Iyeyasu ordered the Shogun to be chosen. He was connected by marriage with the families of the Emperor and the highest Kuges in Miako, and with the wealthiest Daimios. In power the Mito family thus ranked high among the Daimios. Among the scholars the Prince of Mito was popular. The prestige of his great ancestor, the compiler of Dai-Nihon-Shi, had not yet died out. The Prince of Mito was thus naturally looked up to

[1] Given also in Kai-Koku Simatsu, p. 166; Ansei-Kiji, pp. 219, 220.

by the scholars as the man of right principles and of noble ideas. A shrewd, clever, and scheming old man, the Prince of Mito now became the defender of the cause of the Emperor and the mouthpiece of the conservative party.

At the head of the Bakufu party was a man of iron and fertile resources, Ii Kamon No Kami. He was the Daimio of Hikone, a castled town and fief on Lake Biwa, in Mino. His revenue was small, being only three hundred and fifty thousand koku. But in position and power none in the empire could rival him. He was the head of the Fudai Daimios. His family was called the Dodai or foundation-stone of the power of the Tokugawa dynasty. His ancestor, Ii Nawo Massa, had been lieutenant-general and right-hand man of Iyeyas. Ii Kamon No Kami, owing to the mental infirmity of the reigning Shogun, had lately become his regent. Bold, ambitious, able, and unscrupulous, Ii was the Richelieu of Japan. From this time on till his assassination on March 23, 1860, he virtually ruled the empire, and, in direct contravention to the imperial will, negotiated with foreign nations, as we have seen, for the opening of ports for trade with them. He was styled the "swaggering prime minister," and his name was long pronounced with contempt and odium. Lately, however, his good name has been res-cued and his fame restored by the noble effort of an able writer, Mr. Saburo Shimada.[1]   But this able prime minister fell on March 23, 1860, by the sword of Mito ronins, who alleged, as the pretext of their crime, that " Ii Kamon No Kami had insulted the imperial decree and, careless of the misery of the people, but making foreign intercourse his chief aim, had opened ports."   "The position of the government upon the death of the regent was that of helpless inactivity. The sudden removal of the foremost man of the empire was as the removal of the fly-wheel from a piece of complicated machinery. The whole empire stood aghast, expecting and fearing some great political convulsion."[2]

---

[1] Life of Ii Nawosuke Tokyo, 1888.   [2] Dickson's Japan, p. 454.

The Shogun began to make a compromise to unite the Emperor's power and the Shogun's, by taking the sister of the Emperor for his wife.

Meanwhile great events were taking place in the southern corner of Kiushiu and on the promontory of Shikoku, events which were to effect great changes in men's ideas. These were the bombardments of Kagoshima and of Shimonosheki, the first on August 11, 1863, the second on September 5, 1864. I shall not dwell here on the injustice of these barbarous and heathenish acts of the so-called civilized and Christian nations; for I am not writing a political pamphlet. But impartially let us note the great effects of these bombardments.

1. These conflicts showed on a grand but sad scale the weakness of the Daimios, even the most powerful of them, and, on the other hand, the power of the foreigners and their rifled cannon and steamers. The following Japanese memorandum expresses this point : "Satsuma's eyes were opened since the fight of Kagoshima, and affairs appeared to him in a new light; he changed in favor of foreigners, and thought now of making his country powerful and completing his armaments."[1]

The Emperor also wrote in a rather pathetic tone to the Shogun touching the relative strength of the Japanese and the foreigners: "I held a council the other day with my military nobility (Daimios and nobles), but unfortunately inured to the habits of peace, which for more than two hundred years has existed in our country, we are unable to exclude and subdue our foreign enemies by the forcible means of war. . . . .

"If we compare our Japanese ships of war and cannon to those of the barbarians, we feel certain that they are not sufficient to inflict terror upon the foreign barbarians, and are also insufficient to make the splendor of Japan shine in

---

[1] American Executive Document, Diplomatic Correspondence, Part 3, 1865–66, p. 233, 1st Sess. 39th Cong.

foreign countries. I should think that we only should make ourselves ridiculous in the eyes of the barbarians."[1]

From the time of the bombardment, Satsuma and Choshiu began to introduce European machinery and inventions, to employ skilled Europeans to teach them, and to send their young men to Europe and America.

II. These bombardments showed the necessity of national union. Whether she would repel or receive the foreigner, Japan must present a united front. To this end, great change in the internal constitution of the empire was needed ; the internal resources of the nation had to be gathered into a common treasury ; the police and the taxes had to be recognized as national, not as belonging to petty local chieftains ; the power of the feudal lords had to be broken in order to reconstitute Japan as a single strong state under a single head. These are the ideas which led the way to the Restoration of 1868. Thus the bombardments of Kagoshima and Shimonosheki may be said to have helped indirectly in the Restoration of that year. But before we proceed to the history of the Restoration, let us examine what were the great Councils of Kuges and Daimios, which were sometimes convened during the period from 1857 to 1868.

The Council of Kuges was occasionally convened by the order of the Emperor. It was composed of the princes of the blood, nobles, and courtiers. The Council of Daimios was now and then summoned either by the Emperor or by the Shogun. It was composed mostly of the Daimios. These councils were like the Witenagemot of England, formed of the wise and influential men of the kingdom. As the Daimios had far more weight in the political scale of the realm than the Kuges, so the council of the Daimios was of far more importance than that of the Kuges. But it must not be understood that these councils were regular meetings held in the modern parliamentary way ; nor that they had anything

---

[1] American Executive Document, Diplomatic Correspondence, Part 3, 1864–65, p. 502, 2d Sess. 38th Cong.

like the powers of the British Parliament or of the American Congress. These councils of Japan were called into spasmodic life simply by the necessity of the time. They were held either at the court of Kioto or that of Yedo, or at other places appointed for the purpose. The Kuges or Daimios assembled rather in an informal way, measured by modern parliamentary procedure, but in accordance with the court etiquette of the time, whose most minute regulations and rules have often embarrassed and plagued the modern ministers accredited to the court of the Emperor. Then these councils proceeded to discuss the burning questions of the day, among which the most prominent was, of course, the foreign policy. The earliest instance of the meeting of the Council of Kuges was immediately after the news of Perry's arrival had reached the court of Kioto. " Upon this," says the author of Genje Yume Monogatari, "the Emperor was much disturbed, and called a council, which was attended by a number of princes of the blood and Kuges, and much violent language was uttered."

From this time on we meet often with the record of these councils.[1] A native chronicler records that on the 29th day of the 12th month of 1857 "a meeting of all Daimios (present in Yedo) was held in the Haku-sho-in, a large hall in the castle of Yedo. The deliberations were not over till two o'clock on the morning of the 30th."

Soon after this the Emperor ordered the Shogun to come to Kioto with all the Daimios and ascertain the opinion of the country. But the Shogun did not come, so the Emperor sent his envoy, Ohara Sammi, and called the meeting of the Daimios at Yedo in 1862, in which the noted Shimadzu Saburo was also present.

In 1864 the council of Daimios was again held, and Minister Pruyn, in his letter to Mr. Seward, bears witness of the proceeding : " It is understood the great council of

---

[1] See Ansei-Kiji, pages 1, 3, 57, 59, 61, 174, 192, 352 ; Bosin-Simatsu, Vol. II., pp. 4, 69 ; Vol. III., pp. 379, 414 ; Vol. IV., pp. 121, 152.

Daimios is again in session ; that the question of the foreign policy of the government is again under consideration, and that the opposite parties are pretty evenly balanced."[1]

From this time the council of Daimios was held every year, sometimes many times in the year, till the Revolution of 1868. These examples will suffice to show the nature and purpose of these councils of Kuges and Daimios. Let us next consider how these councils originated.

The political development of Japan gives another illustration of one of the truths which Mr. Herbert Spencer unfolds in his Principles of Sociology. " Everywhere the wars between societies," says he, " originate governmental structures, and are causes of all such improvements in those structures as increase the efficiency of corporate action against environing societies."[2]

Experience has shown that representative government is the most efficient in securing the corporate action of the various members of the body politic against foreign enemies. When a country is threatened with foreign invasion, when the corporate action of its citizens against their enemy is needed, it becomes an imperative necessity to consult public opinion. In such a time centralization is needed. Hence the first move of Japan after the advent of foreigners was to bring the scattered parts of the country together and unite them under one head.

Japan had hitherto no formidable foreign enemy on her shores. So her governmental system—the regulating system of the social organism—received no impetus for self-development. But as soon as a formidable people, either as allies or foes, appeared on the scene in 1853, we immediately see the remarkable change in the state system of regulation in Japan. It became necessary to consult public opinion. Councils of Kuges and Daimios and meetings of Samurai sprung forth spontaneously.

---

[1] American Executive Document, Diplomatic Correspondence, Part 3, 1864–65, p. 486, 2d Sess. 38th Cong.

[2] Principles of Sociology, p. 540.

I believe, with Guizot, that the germ of representative government was not necessarily "in the woods of Germany," as Montesquieu asserts, or in the Witenagemot of England; that the glory of having a free government is not necessarily confined to the Aryan family or to its more favored branch, the Anglo-Saxons. I believe that the seed of representative government is implanted in the very nature of human society and of the human mind. When the human mind and the social organism reach a certain stage of development, when they are placed in such an environment as to call forth a united and harmonious action of the body politic, when education is diffused among the masses and every member of the community attains a certain degree of his individuality and importance, when the military form of society transforms itself into the industrial, then the representative idea of government springs forth naturally and irresistibly. And no tyrant, no despot, can obstruct the triumphal march of liberty.

Whatever may be said about the soundness of the above speculation, it is certain that in the great councils of Kuges and Daimios and in the discussions of the Samurai, which the advent of the foreigners called into being, lay the germ of the future constitutional parliament of Japan.

CHAPTER II.

The Restoration.

In the last chapter we have noticed what a commotion had been caused in Japan by the sudden advent of Commodore Perry, how the councils of Kuges and Daimios were called into spontaneous life by the dread of foreigners and by the sense of national weakness, and how the bombardments of Kagoshima and Shimonosheki tested these fears and taught the necessity of national union. I have remarked that free government is not necessarily the sole heritage of the Aryan race, but that the presence of foreigners, the change of the military form of society into the industrial form, the increase in importance of the individual in the community, are sure to breed a free and representative system of government.

In the following chapter we shall see the downfall of the Shogunate, the restoration of the imperial power to its pristine vigor, and the destruction of feudalism.

"The study of constitutional history is essentially a tracing of causes and consequences," says Bishop Stubbs, "not the collection of a multitude of facts and views, but the piecing of links of a perfect chain."

I shall therefore not dwell upon the details of the events which led to the downfall of the Shogunate, but immediately enter into an inquiry concerning the causes.

Three causes led to the final overthrow of the Shogunate:

I. The Revival of Learning. The last half of the eighteenth and the first half of the present century witnessed in Japan an unusual intellectual activity. The long peace and prosperity of the country under the rule of the Tokugawa dynasties had fostered in every way the growth of literature and

art. The Shoguns, from policy or from taste, either to find
a harmless vent for the restless spirit of the Samura or from
pure love of learning, have been constant patrons of literature. The Daimios, too, as a means of spending their leisure
hours when they were not out hawking or revelling with
their mistresses, gave no inattentive ear to the readings and
lectures of learned men. Each Daimioate took pride in
the number and fame of her own learned sons. Thus
throughout the country eminent scholars arose. With them
a new era of literature dawned upon the land. The new
literature changed its tone. Instead of the servility, faint
suggestiveness, and restrained politeness characteristic of the
literature from the Gen-hei period to the first half of the
Tokugawa period, that of the Revival Era began to wear a
bolder and freer aspect. History came to be recorded with
more truthfulness and boldness than ever before.

But as the ancient histories were studied and the old constitution was brought into light, the real nature of the Shogunate
began to reveal itself. To the eyes of the historians it became
clear that the Shogunate was nothing but a military usurpation, sustained by fraud and corruption; that the Emperor,
who was at that time, in plain words, imprisoned at the court
of Kioto, was the real source of power and honor. "If this
be the case, what ought we do?" was the natural question of
these loyal subjects of the Emperor. The natural conclusion
followed: the military usurper must be overthrown and the
rightful ruler recognized. This was the sum and substance of
the political programme of the Imperialists. The first sound
of the trumpet against the Shogunate rose from the learned
hall of the Prince of Mito, Komon. He, with the assistance
of a host of scholars, finished his great work, the Dai Nihon
Shi, or History of Japan, in 1715. It was not printed till
1851, but was copied from hand to hand by eager students,
like the Bible by the medieval monks, or the works of
Plato and Aristotle by the Humanists. The Dai Nihon Shi
soon became a classic, and had such an influence in restoring

the power of the Emperor that Mr. Ernest Satow justly calls its composer " the real author of the movement which culminated in the revolution of 1868." The voice of the Prince of Mito was soon caught up by the more celebrated scholar Rai Sanyo (1780–1833). A poet, an historian, and a zealous patriot, Rai Sanyo was the Arndt of Japan. He outlined in his Nihon Guai Shi the rise and fall of the Minister of State and the Shoguns, and with satire, invective, and the enthusiasm of a patriot, urged the unlawfulness of the usurpation of the imperial power by these mayors of the palace. In his Sei-Ki, or political history of Japan, he traced the history of the imperial family, and mourned with characteristic pathos the decadence of the imperial power. The labors of these historians and scholars bore in time abundant fruit. Some of their disciples became men of will and action : Sakuma Shozan, Yoshida Toraziro, Gesho, Yokoi Heishiro, and later Saigo, Okubo, Kido, and hosts of others, who ultimately realized the dreams of their masters. Out of the literary seed which scholars like Rai Sanyo spread broad-cast over the country thus grew hands of iron and hearts of steel. This process shows how closely related are history and politics, and affords another illustration of the signifi-cance of the epigrammatic expression of Professor Freeman : " History is past politics, and politics present history."

II. Another tributary stream which helped to swell the tide flowing toward the Emperor was the revival of Shinto-ism. The revival of learning is sure to be followed by the revival of religion. This is shown in the history of the Reformation in Europe, which was preceded by the revival of learning. Since the expulsion of Christianity from Japan in the sixteenth century, which was effected more from political than religious motives, laissez-faire was the steadfast policy of the Japanese rulers toward religious matters. The founder of the Tokugawa dynasty had laid down in his "Legacy" the policy to be pursued by his descendants. "Now any one of the people," says Iyeyasu, "can adhere to which (religion) he pleases (except the Christian); and there must be no wrangling among sects to the disturbance of the peace of the Empire." Thus while the people in the West, who worshipped the Prince of Peace, in his abused name were cutting each other's throat, destroying each other's property, torturing and proselyting by rack and flames, the islanders on the West Pacific coast were enjoying complete religious toleration. Three religions—Shintoism, Buddhism, and Confucianism—lived together in peace. In such a state of unrestricted competition among various religions, the universal law of the survival of the fittest acts freely. Buddhism was the fittest and became the predominant religion. Shintoism was the weakest and sank into helpless desuetude. But with the revival of learning, as Kojiki and other ancient literature were studied with assiduity, Shintoism began to revive. Its cause found worthy defenders in Motoori and Hirata. They are among the greatest Shintoists Japan has ever seen.

Now, according to Shintoism, Japan is a holy land. It was made by the gods, whose lineal descendant is the Emperor. Hence he must be revered and worshipped as a god. This is the substance of Shintoism. The political bearing of such a doctrine upon the then existing status of the country is apparent. The Emperor, who is a god, the fountain of all virtue, honor, and authority, is now a prisoner at the court of Kioto, under the iron hand of the Tokugawa Shoguns. This state of impiety and irreverence can never be tolerated by the devout Shintoists. The Shogun must be dethroned and the Emperor raised to power. Here the line of arguments of the Shintoists meets with that of the scholars we have noted above. Thus both scholars and Shintoists have converted themselves into politicians who have at heart the restoration of the Emperor.

III. Another cause which led to the overthrow of the Shogunate was the jealousy and cupidity of the Southern Daimios. Notably among them were the Daimios of Satsuma,

Choshiu, Tosa, and Hizen. Their ancestors "had of old held equal rank and power with Iyeyasu, until the fortunes of war turned against them. They had been overcome by force, or had sullenly surrendered in face of overwhelming odds. Their adherence to the Tokugawas was but nominal, and only the strong pressure of superior power was able to wring from them a haughty semblance of obedience. They chafed perpetually under the rule of one who was in reality a vassal like themselves."[1] They now saw in the rising tide of public sentiment against the Tokugawa Shogunate a rare opportunity of accomplishing their cherished aim. They lent their arms and money for the support of the patriots in carrying out their plan. Satsuma and Choshiu became the rendezvous of eminent scholars and zealous patriots. And in the council-halls of Satsuma and Choshiu were hatched the plots which were soon to overthrow the effete Shogunate.

Thus everything was ready for the revolution of 1868 before Perry came. We saw the Shogun, under the bombastic title of Tycoon, in spite of the remonstrance of the Emperor and his court, conclude a treaty with Perry at Kanagawa in 1854. Here at last was found a pretext for the Imperialists to raise arms against the Shogun. The Shogun or his ministers had no right to make treaties with foreigners. Such an act was, in the eyes of the patriots, heinous treason. The cry of "Destroy the Shogunate and raise the Emperor to his proper throne!" rang from one end of the empire to the other. The constant disturbance of the country, the difficulty of foreign intercourse, the sense of necessity of a single and undoubted authority over the land, and the outcry of the Samurai thus raised against the Shogun, finally led to his resignation on November 19, 1867. His letter of resignation, in the form of a manifesto to the Daimios, runs thus:

"A retrospect of the various changes through which the empire has passed shows us that after the decadence of the monarchical authority, power passed into the hands of the

---

[1] The Mikado's Empire. Griffis, p. 301.

Minister of State; that by the wars of 1156 to 1159 the governmental power came into the hands of the military class. My ancestor received greater marks of confidence than any before him, and his descendants have succeeded him for more than two hundred years. Though I perform the same duties, the objects of government and the penal laws have not been attained, and it is with feelings of greatest humiliation that I find myself obliged to ackowledge my own want of virtue as the cause of the present state of things. Moreover, our intercourse with foreign powers becomes daily more extensive, and our foreign policy cannot be pursued unless directed by the whole power of the country.

"If, therefore, the old régime be changed and the governmental authority be restored to the imperial court, if the councils of the whole empire be collected and the wise decisions received, and if we unite with all our heart and with all our strength to protect and maintain the empire, it will be able to range itself with the nations of the earth. This comprises our whole duty towards our country.

"However, if you (the Daimios) have any particular ideas on the subject, you may state them without reserve."[1]

The resignation of the Shogun was accepted by the Emperor by the following imperial order, issued on the 10th day of the 12th month: "It has pleased the Emperor to dismiss the present Shogun, at his request, from the office of Shogun."

As to the full intent and motive of the Shogun in resigning his power, let him further speak himself. In the interview of the British minister, Sir Harry S. Parkes, and the French minister, M. Leon Roches, with the Shogun, it is stated that he said: "I became convinced last autumn that the country would no longer be successfully governed while the power was divided between the Emperor and myself. The country had two centres, from which orders of an opposite nature proceeded. Thus, in the matter of the opening

---

[1] American Executive Document, Diplomatic Correspondence, 1867, Part II., p. 78, 2d Sess. 40th Cong. See also Bosin-Simatsu, Vol. I., p. 2.

of Hiogo and Osako, which I quote as an example of this conflict of authority, I was myself convinced that the stipulations of the treaties must be observed, but the assent of the Emperor to my representations on this subject was given reluctantly. I therefore, for the good of my country, informed the Emperor that I resigned the governing power, with the understanding that an assembly of Daimios was convened for the purpose of deciding in what manner, and by whom, the government in future should be carried on. In acting thus, I sunk my own interests and power handed down to me by my ancestors, in the more important interests of the country.[1] . . . .

" My policy, from the commencement, has been to determine this question of the future form of government in a peaceful manner, and it is in pursuance of the same object that, instead of opposing force by force, I have retired from the scene of dispute. . . . .

"As to who is the sovereign of Japan, it is a question on which no one in Japan can entertain a doubt. The Emperor is the sovereign. My object from the first has been to take the will of the nation as to the future government. If the nation should decide that I ought to resign my powers, I am prepared to resign them for the good of my country. . . . .

" I have no other motive but the following : With an honest love for my country and the people, I resigned the governing power which I inherited from my ancestors, and with the mutual understanding that I should assemble all the nobles of the empire to discuss the question disinterestedly, and adopting the opinion of the majority, decide upon the reformation of the national constitution, I left the matter in the hands of the imperial court."[2]

Thus was the Shogunate overthrown and the Restoration effected. The civil war which soon followed need not detain

---

[1] American Executive Document, Diplomatic Correspondence, Vol. I., 1868–69, p. 620, 3d Sess. 40th Cong.

[2] American Executive Document, Diplomatic Correspondence, Vol. I., 1868–69, p. 622, 3d Sess. 40th Cong.

us, for the war itself had no great consequence as regards the constitutional development of the country.

Let us now consider the form of the new government. It is essentially that which prevailed in Japan before the development of feudalism. It is modelled on the form of government of the Osei era.

The new government was composed of:

1. Sosai ("Supreme Administrator"). He was assisted by Fuku, or Vice-Sosai. The Sosai resembled the British Premier, was the head of the chief council of the government.

2. Gijio, or "Supreme Council," whose function was to discuss all questions and suggest the method of their settlement to the Sosai. It was composed of ten members, five of whom were selected from the list of Kuges and five from the great Daimios.

3. Sanyo, or "Associate Council." They were subordinate officers, and were selected from the Daimios as well as from the retainers. This council finally came to have great influence, and ultimately transformed itself into the present cabinet.

The government was divided into eight departments:

1. The Sosai Department. This soon changed into Daijo-Kuan.

2. Jingi-Jimu-Kioku, or Department of the Shinto Religion. This department had charge of the Shinto temples, priests, and festivals.

3. Naikoku-Jimu-Kioku, or Department of Home Affairs. This department had charge of the capital and the five home provinces, of land and water transport in all the provinces, of post-towns and post-roads, of barriers and fairs, and of the governors of castles, towns, ports, etc.

4. Guaikoku-Jimu-Kioku, or Department of Foreign Affairs. This department had charge of foreign relations, treaties, trade, recovery of lands, and sustenance of the people.

5. Gumbu-Jimu-Kioku, or War Department. This department had charge of the naval and military forces, drilling, protection of the Emperor, and military defences in general.

6. Kuaikei-Jimu-Kioku, or Department of Finance. This
department had charge of the registers of houses and popula-
tion, of tariff and taxes, money, corn, accounts, tribute, build-
ing and repairs, salaries, public storehouses, and internal
trade.

. 7. Keiho-Jimu-Kioku, or Judicial Department. This
department had charge of the censorate, of inquisitions,
arrests, trials, and the penal laws in general.

8. Seido-Jimu-Kioku, or Legislative Department. This
department had charge of the superintendence of offices,
enactments, sumptuary regulations, appointments, and all
other laws and regulations,   .

" It is easy to destroy, but difficult to construct," is an old
adage of statesmen. The truth of this utterance was soon
realized by the leaders of the new government.

The first thing which the new government had to settle was
its attitude toward foreign nations. The leaders of the government who had once opposed with such vehemence, as we
have seen, the foreign policy of the Tokugawa Shogun, now
that he had been overthrown, urged the necessity of amicable
relations with foreign powers in the following memorable
memorial[1] to the Dai-jo-Kuan (Government):

" The undersigned, servants of the Crown, respectfully
believe that from ancient times decisions upon important
questions concerning the welfare of the empire were arrived
at after consideration of the actual political condition and its
necessities, and that thus results were obtained, not of mere
temporary brilliancy, but which bore good fruits in all
time. . . . .

"Among other pressing duties of the present moment we
venture to believe it to be pre-eminently important to set the
question of foreign intercourse in a clear light.

[1] Translation from the Kioto Government Gazette of March, 1868. It
is given in Diplomatic Correspondence of the U. S. A., 3d Sess. 40th Cong.,
Vol. I., 1868–69, p. 725.

"His Majesty's object in creating the office of administrator of foreign affairs, and selecting persons to fill it, and otherwise exerting himself in that direction, has been to show the people of his empire in what light to look on this matter, and we have felt the greatest pleasure in thinking that the imperial glory would now be made to shine forth before all nations. An ancient proverb says that 'Men's minds resemble each other as little as their faces,' nor have the upper and lower classes been able, up to the present, to hold with confidence a uniform opinion. It gives us some anxiety to feel that perhaps we may be following the bad example of the Chinese, who, fancying themselves alone great and worthy of respect, and despising foreigners as little better than beasts, have come to suffer defeats at their hands and to have it lorded over themselves by those foreigners.

"It appears to us, therefore, after mature reflection, that the most important duty we have at present is for high and low to unite harmoniously in understanding the condition of the age, in effecting a national reformation and commencing a great work, and that for this reason it is of the greatest necessity that we determine upon the attitude to be observed towards this question.

"Hitherto the empire has held itself aloof from other countries and is ignorant of the affairs of the world; the only object sought has been to give ourselves the least trouble, and by daily retrogression we are in danger of falling under foreign rule.

"By travelling to foreign countries and observing what good there is in them, by comparing their daily progress, the universality of enlightened government, of a sufficiency of military defences, and of abundant food for the people among them, with our present condition, the causes of prosperity and degeneracy may be plainly traced. . . . .

"Of late years the question of expelling the barbarians has been constantly agitated, and one or two Daimios have tried to expel them, but it is unnecessary to prove that this was more than the strength of a single clan could accomplish. . . . .

"However, in order to restore the fallen fortunes of the empire and to make the imperial dignity respected abroad, it is necessary to make a firm resolution, and to get rid of the narrow-minded ideas which have prevailed hitherto. We pray that the important personages of the court will open their eyes and unite with those below them in establishing relations of amity in a single-minded manner, and that our deficiencies being supplied with what foreigners are superior in, an enduring government be established for future ages. Assist the Emperor in forming his decision wisely and in understanding the condition of the empire; let the foolish argument which has hitherto styled foreigners dogs and goats and barbarians be abandoned; let the court ceremonies, hitherto imitated from the Chinese, be reformed, and the foreign representatives be bidden to court in the manner prescribed by the rules current amongst all nations; and let this be publicly notified throughout the country, so that the countless people may be taught what is the light in which they are to regard this subject. This is our most earnest prayer, presented with all reverence and humility.

> ECHIZEN SAISHO,
> TOSA SAKIO NO SHOSHO,
> NAGATO SHOSHO,
> SATSUMA SHOSHO,
> AKI SHOSHO,
> HOSO KAWA UKIO DAIBU."

The advice of these notables was well received. A formal invitation to an audience with the Emperor was extended to the foreign ambassadors. They soon accepted the invitation. Their appearance in the old anti-foreign city of Kioto, before the personage who was considered by the masses as divine, was significant. It put an end to the all-absorbing, all-perplexing theme of the day. The question of foreign policy was settled.

The next act of the statesmen of the Restoration was to sweep away the abuses of the court, and to establish the basis of a firm internal administration. The most effectual means of accomplishing this, it seemed to the sagacious statesmen, was to move the court from the place where those abuses had their roots. Ichizo Okubo,[1] a guiding spirit of the Restoration, presented the following memorial to the Emperor:

"'The most pressing of your Majesty's pressing duties at the present moment is not to look at the empire alone and judge carelessly by appearances, but to consider carefully the actual state of the whole world; to reform the inveterate and slothful habits induced during several hundred years, and to give union to the nation. . . . .

"Hitherto the person whom we designate the sovereign has lived behind a screen, and, as if he were different from other human beings, has not been seen by more than a very limited number of Kuge; and as his heaven-conferred office of father to his people has been thereby unfulfilled, it is necessary that his office should be ascertained in accordance with this fundamental principle, and then the laws governing internal affairs may be established. . . . .

"In the present period of reformation and restoration of the government to its ancient monarchical form, the way to carry out the resolution of imitating the example of Japanese sages, and of surpassing the excellent governments of foreign nations, is to change the site of the capital. . . . .

"Osako is the fittest place for the capital. . . . . For the conduct of foreign relations, for enriching the country and strengthening its military power, for adopting successful means of offense and defense, for establishing an army and navy, the place is peculiarly fitted by its position. . . . . I most humbly pray your Majesty to open your eyes and make this reform. . . . .

OKUBO ICHIZO."[2]

---

[1] He afterwards changed his name into Toshimitsu Okubo.

[2] Translation is given in American Executive Document, Diplomatic Correspondence, Vol. I., 1868-69, p. 728, 3d Sess. 40th Cong.

The result of the memorial was the ultimate removal of the seat of government from Kioto to Yedo, which afterwards changed its name to Tokio, meaning eastern capital.

But the most important event of the Restoration, from the constitutional point of view, was the charter oath of five articles, taken by the present Emperor on the 17th of April, 1869, before the court and the assembly of Daimios. These articles were in substance as follows:

1. A deliberative assembly should be formed, and all measures be decided by public opinion.

2. The principles of social and political economics should be diligently studied by both the superior and inferior classes of our people.

3. Every one in the community shall be assisted to persevere in carrying out his will for all good purposes.

4. All the old absurd usages of former times should be disregarded, and the impartiality and justice displayed in the workings of nature be adopted as a basis of action.

5. Wisdom and ability should be sought after in all quarters of the world for the purpose of firmly establishing the foundations of the empire.

The Emperor's promise henceforth became the watchword of the nation.

And this resolution to form a deliberative assembly was soon put into practice. In 1869 was convened the Kogisho or "Parliament," as Sir Harry Parkes translates it in his despatch to the Earl of Clarendon. But before we proceed to the description of the nature and working of the Kogisho it is necessary to state that this plan had been already suggested by the Shogunate. A proclamation of the Shogun Keiki, issued on February 20, 1868, says: "As it is proper to determine the principle of the constitution of Japan with due regard to the wishes of the majority, I have resigned the supreme power to the Emperor's court, and advised that the opinions of all the Daimios should be taken . . . On examination of my household affairs (the administration of Sho-

gun's territories), many irregularities may exist which may
dissatisfy the people, and which I therefore greatly deplore.
Hence I intend to establish a Kogijio and to accept the
opinion of the majority. Any one, therefore, who has an
opinion to express may do so at that place and be free of
apprehension."[1]

But this attempt of the Shogun to establish a sort of
Parliament came to an end with his fall. This idea, however, was transmitted through the Shogunate officials to the
government of the Restoration. In fact, this idea of con-
sulting public opinion was, as I have repeatedly said, in the
air. The leaders of the new government all felt, as one of them
said to Messrs. F. O. Adams and Ernest Satow, that "the
only way to allay the jealousies hitherto existing between
several of the most powerful clans, and to ensure a solid and
lasting union of conflicting interests, was to search for the
nearest approach to an ideal constitution among those of
Western countries . . . that the opinion of the majority was
the only criterion of a public measure."[2]

Sir Harry Parkes was right when he told the Earl of Clarendon that "the establishment of such an institution (the
Kogisho) formed one of the first objects of the promoters of
the recent revolution."[3]

The Kogisho was opened on the 18th of April, 1869,[4] and
the following message[5] from the throne was then delivered :

. "Being on the point of visiting our eastern capital, we
have convened the nobles of our court and the various
princes in order to consult them upon the means of establishing the foundations of peaceful government. The laws
and institutions are the basis of government. The petitions

[1] American Executive Document, Diplomatic Correspondence, Vol. I.,
1868–69, p. 687, 3d Sess. 40th Cong.
[2] F. O. Adams' History of Japan, Vol. II., p. 128.
[3] English State Papers, Vol. LXX., 1870, p. 9.
[4] 29th of the 2d month in the second year of Meiji, according to the old
calendar.
[5] Translation is given in English State Papers, Vol. LXX., 1871, p. 12.

of the people at large cannot be lightly decided. It has been reported to us that brief rules and regulations have been fixed upon for the Parliament, and it seems good to us that the House should be opened at once. We exhort you to respect the laws of the House, to lay aside all private and selfish considerations, to conduct your debates with minuteness and firmness ; above all things, to take the laws of our ancestors as ' basis,' and adapt yourselves to the feelings of men and to the spirit of the times. Distinguish clearly between those matters which are of immediate importance and those which may be delayed ; between things which are less urgent and those which are pressing. In your several capacities argue with careful attention. When the results of your debate are communicated to us it shall be our duty to confirm them."

The Kogisho was composed mostly of the retainers of the Daimios, for the latter, having no experience of the earnest business of life, " were not eager to devote themselves to the labors of an onerous and voluntary office." Akidzuki Ukio No Suke was appointed President of the Kogisho.

The object of the Kogisho was to enable the government to sound public opinion on the various topics of the day, and to obtain the assistance of the country in the work of legislation by ascertaining whether the projects of the government were likely to be favorably received.

The Kogisho, like the Councils of Kuges and Daimios, was nothing but an experiment, a mere germ of a deliberative assembly, which only time and experience could bring to maturity. Still Kogisho was an advance over the council of Daimios. It had passed the stage resembling a mere deliberative meeting or quiet Quaker conference, where, for hours perhaps, nobody opens his mouth. It now bore an aspect of a political club meeting. But it was a quiet, peaceful, obedient debating society. It has left the record of its abortive undertakings in the " Kogisho Nishi " or journal of " Parliament." The Kogisho was dissolved in the year of its birth.   And the indifference of the public about its dissolution proves how small an influence it really had.

But a greater event than the dissolution of the Kogisho was pending before the public gaze.   This was the abolition of feudalism, which we shall consider in the next chapter.

CHAPTER III.

THE ABOLITION OF FEUDALISM.

The measure to abolish feudalism was much discussed in the Kogisho before its dissolution. Prince Akidzuki, President of the Kogisho, had sent in the following memorial:

" After the government had been returned by the Tokugawa family into the hands of the Emperor, the calamity of war ensued, and the excellence of the newly established administration has not yet been able to perfect itself; if this continues, I am grieved to think how the people will give up their allegiance. Happily, the eastern and northern provinces have already been pacified and the country at large has at last recovered from its troubles. The government of the Emperor is taking new steps every day; this is truly a noble thing for the country. And yet when I reflect, I see that although there are many who profess loyalty, none have yet shown proof of it. The various princes have used their lands and their people for their own purposes; different laws have obtained in different places; the civil and criminal codes have been various in the various provinces. The clans have been called the screen of the country, but in truth they have caused its division. The internal relations having been confused, the strength of the country has been disunited and severed. How can our small country of Japan enter into fellowship with the countries beyond the sea? How can she hold up an example of a flourishing country? Let those who wish to show their faith and loyalty act in the following manner, that they may firmly establish the foundations of the Imperial Government:

1. Let them restore the territories which they have received from the Emperor and return to a constitutional and undivided country.

2. Let them abandon their titles, and under the name of Kuazoku (persons of honor) receive such small properties as may suffice for their wants.

3. Let the officers of the clans abandoning that title call themselves officers of the Emperor, receiving property equal to that which they have hitherto held.

Let these three important measures be adopted forthwith, that the empire may be raised on a basis imperishable for ages . . . 2nd year of Meiji (1869).

(Signed)   AKIDZUKI UKIO NO SUKE."[1]

But politics is not an easy game—a game which a pedant or a sentimental scholar or an orator can leisurely play. It has to deal with passions, ambitions, and selfish interests of men, as well as with the moral and intellectual conscious-ness of the people. Tongue and pen wield, undoubtedly, a great influence in shaping the thought of the nation and impressing them with the importance of any political measure. But the tongue is as sounding brass and the pen as useless steel unless they are backed by force and money. Even in such a country as England, where tongue and pen seem to reign supreme, a prime minister before he forms his cabinet has to be closeted for hours with Mr. Rothschild. Fortunately this important measure of abolishing feudalism, which a few patriots had secretly plotted and which the scholars had noised abroad, was taken up first by the most powerful and wealthy Daimios of the country.

In the following noted memorial, after reviewing the polit-ical history of Japan during the past few hundred years, these Daimios said : " Now the great Government has been newly restored and the Emperor himself undertakes the direction of affairs. This is, indeed, a rare and mighty event. We have the name (of an Imperial Government), we must also have the fact. Our first duty is to illustrate our faithfulness and to prove our loyalty. When the line of

---

[1] Translation given in the English State Papers.

Tokugawa arose it divided the country amongst its kinsfolk, and there were many who founded the fortunes of their families upon it. They waited not to ask whether the lands and men that they received were the gift of the Emperor; for ages they continued to inherit these lands until this day. Others said that their possessions were the prize of their spears and bows, as if they had entered storehouses and stolen the treasure therein, boasting to the soldiers by whom they were surrounded that they had done this regardless of their lives. Those who enter storehouses are known by all men to be thieves, but those who rob lands and steal men are not looked upon with suspicion. How are loyalty and faith confused and destroyed!

" The place where we live is the Emperor's land and the food which we eat is grown by the Emperor's men. How can we make it our own? We now reverently offer up the list of our possessions and men, with the prayer that the Emperor will take good measures for rewarding those to whom reward is due and for taking from those to whom punishment is due. Let the imperial orders be issued for altering and remodelling the territories of the various clans. Let the civil and penal codes, the military laws down to the rules for uniform and the construction of engines of war, all proceed from the Emperor; let all the affairs of the empire, great and small, be referred to him."

This memorial was signed by the Daimios of Kago, Hizen, Satsuma, Choshiu, Tosa, and some other Daimios of the west. But the real author of the memorial is believed to have been Kido, the brain of the Restoration.

Thus were the fiefs of the most powerful and most wealthy Daimios voluntarily offered to the Emperor. The other Daimios soon followed the example of their colleagues. And the feudalism which had existed in Japan for over eight centuries was abolished by the following laconic imperial decree of August, 1871 :

" The clans are abolished, and prefectures are established in their places."

This rather off-hand way of destroying an institution, whose overthrow in Europe required the combined efforts of ambitious kings and emperors, of free cities, of zealous religious sects, and cost centuries of bloodshed, has been made a matter of much comment in the West. One writer exclaims, " History does not record another instance where changes of such magnitude ever occurred within so short a time, and it is astonishing that it only required eleven words to destroy the ambition and power of a proud nobility that had with imperious will directed the destiny of Japan for more than five hundred years." [1]

But when we examine closely the circumstances which led to the overthrow of feudalism and the influences which acted upon it, we cannot but regard it as the natural terminus of the political flood which was sweeping over the country. When such a revolution of thought as that expressed in the proclamation of 1868 had taken place in the minds of the leaders of society, when contact with foreigners had fostered the necessity of national union, when the spirit of loyalty of the Samurai had changed to loyalty to his Emperor, when his patriotic devotion to his province had changed to patriotic devotion to his country, then it became apparent that the petty social organization, which was antagonistic to these national principles, would soon be crushed.

If there is any form of society which is diametrically opposed to the spirit of national union, of liberal thought, of free intercourse, it is feudal society. A monarchical or a democratic society encourages the spirit of union, but feudal society must, from its very nature, smother it. Seclusion is the parent of feudalism. In our enlightened and progressive century seclusion is no longer possible. Steam and electricity alone would have been sufficient to destroy our Japanese feudalism. But long before its fall our Japanese feudalism " was an empty shell." Its leaders, the Daimios of provinces, were, with a few exceptions, men of no commanding

---

[1] Consular Report of the U. S. A., No. 75, p. 626.

importance. " The real power in each clan lay in the hands of able men of inferior rank, who ruled their masters." From these men came the present advisers of the Emperor. Their chief object at that time was the thorough unification of Japan. Why, then, should they longer trouble themselves to uphold feudalism, this mother of sectionalism, this colossal sham?

CHAPTER IV.

INFLUENCES THAT SHAPED THE GROWTH OF THE REPRESENTATIVE IDEA OF GOVERNMENT.

We have seen in the last two chapters how the Shogunate and feudalism fell, and how the Meiji government was inaugurated. We have also observed in the memorials of leading statesmen abundant proof of their willingness and zeal to introduce a representative system of government. We have also seen the Kogisho convened and dissolved.

John Stuart Mill has pointed out, in his Representative Government, several social conditions when representative government is inapplicable or unsuitable:

1. When the people are not willing to receive it.
2. When the people are not willing and able to do what is necessary for its preservation.

" Representative institutions necessarily depend for permanence upon the readiness of the people to fight for them in case of their being endangered."

3. When the people are not willing and able to fulfil the duties and discharge the functions which it imposes on them.
4. When the people have not learned the first lesson of obedience.
5. When the people are too passive; when they are ready to submit to tyranny.

Now when we look at the Japan of 1871, even her greatest admirers must admit that she was far from being able to fulfil the social conditions necessary for the success of representative government. Japan was obedient, but too submissive. She had not yet learned the first lesson of freedom, that is, when and how to resist, in the faith that resistance to tyrants is obedience to truth; that the irrepressible kicker against tyranny, as Dr. Wilson observes, is the only true freeman. In her conservative, almost abject submission, Japan was yet unfit for free government. The Japanese people were willing to do almost anything suggested by their Emperor, but they had first to learn what was meant by representative government, "to understand its processes and requirements." The Japanese had to discard many old habits and prejudices, reform many defects of national character, and undergo many stages of moral and mental discipline before they could acclimatize themselves to the free atmosphere of representative institutions. This preparation required a period of little over two decades, and was effected not only through political discipline, but by corresponding development in the moral, intellectual, social, and industrial life of the nation.

I remarked in the beginning that the political activity of a nation is not isolated from other spheres of its activities, but that there is a mutual interchange of action and reaction among the different factors of social life, so that to trace the political life of a nation it is not only necessary to describe the organ through which it acts, the governmental machinery, and the methods by which it is worked, but to know "the forces which move it and direct its course." Now these forces are political as well as non-political. This truth is now generally acknowledged by constitutional writers. Thus, the English author of "The American Commonwealth" devotes over one-third of his second volume to the account of non-political institutions, and says "there are certain non-political institutions, certain aspects of society, certain intellectual or spiritual forces which count for so much in the total life of the country, in the total impression it makes and the hopes for the future which it raises, that they cannot be left unnoticed."[1]

If this be the case in the study of the American commonwealth, it is more so in that of Japanese politics. For

---

[1] The American Commonwealth, Bryce, Vol. I., p. 7.

nowhere else in the history of nations do we see "non-political institutions" exerting such a powerful influence upon the body politic as in New Japan. In this chapter we shall therefore note briefly the growth of so-called "non-political institutions" during a period of about a decade and a half, between 1868 and 1881, and mark their influence upon the development of representative ideas.

I.—MEANS OF COMMUNICATION.

1. *Telegraph.* At the time of the Restoration there was no telegraph in operation, and "for expresses the only available means were men and horses." In 1868 the government began to construct telegraphs, and the report of the Bureau of Statistics in 1881 shows the following increase in each successive year :

Year.	Telegraph Offices.	Miles. Ri Cho.	Number of Telegrams.
1869–1871	8	26.04	19,448
1872	29	33.11	80,639
1873	40	1,099.00	186,448
1874	57	1,333.20	356,539
1875	94	1,904.32	611,866
1876	100	2,214.07	680,939
1877	122	2,827.08	1,045,442
1878	147	3,380.05	1,272,756
1879	195	3,842.31	1,935,320
1880	195	4,484.30	2,168,201

All the more important towns in the country were thus made able to communicate with one another as early as 1880.

In 1879 Japan joined the International Telegraph Convention, and since then she can communicate easily with the great powers of the world through the great submarine cable system. "Compared with the state of ten years ago, when the ignorant people cut down the telegraph poles and severed the wires," exclaims Count Okuma, "we seem rather to have made a century's advance."

2. *Postal System.* " Previous to the Restoration," to quote further from Count Okuma, "with the exception of the posts sent by the Daimios from their residences at the capital to their territories, there was no regularly established post for the general public and private convenience. Letters had to be sent by any opportunity that occurred, and a single letter cost over 25 sen for a distance of 150 ri. But since the Restoration the government for the first time established a general postal service, and in 1879 the length of postal lines was 15,700 ri (nearly 40,000 English miles), and a letter can at any time be sent for two sen to any part of the country. In 1874 we entered the International Postal Convention, and have thus obtained great facilities for communicating with foreign countries."[1]

3. *Railroad.* The first railway Japan ever saw was the model railway constructed by Commodore Perry to excite the curiosity of the people. But it was not until 1870 that the railroad was really introduced into Japan. The first rail was laid on the road between Tokio and Yokohama. This road was opened in 1872. It is 18 miles long. The second line was constructed in 1876, and runs between Hiogo and Kioto via Osako. And the year 1880 saw the opening of the railroad between Kioto and Otsu. This line between Hiogo and Otsu is 58 miles long. So at the end of the period which we are surveying Japan had a railway system of 31 ri and 5 cho (about 78 English miles).

This was nothing but a child-play compared with the railroad activity which the later years brought forth, for now we have a railway system extending over one thousand two hundred miles. But this concerns the later period, so we shall not dwell upon it at present.

4. *Steamers and the coasting trade.* In 1871 the number of

---

[1] A Survey of Financial Policy during Thirteen Years (1868–1880), by Count Okuma.

ships of foreign build was only 74, but by 1878 they had reached 377. The number of vessels of native build in 1876 was 450,000, and in 1878 had reached 460,000.[1]

" Since the Restoration the use of steamers has daily increased, and the inland sea, the lakes and large rivers are now constantly navigated by small steamers employed in the carrying trade."[1]

With the increased facility of communication, commerce and trade were stimulated. In 1869 the total amount of imports and exports was 33,680,000 yen, and in 1879 64,120,000 yen. Imports had grown from 20,780,000 yen to 36,290,000 yen, and exports from 12,909,000 yen to 27,830,000 yen; in the one case showing an advance from 2 to $3\frac{1}{2}$, in the other from 2 to 5.[1]

II.—EDUCATIONAL INSTITUTIONS.

Previous to the Restoration, the schools supported by Daimios and the private schools were few in number; but since that epoch the educational system has been vastly improved, with a resulting increase in the number of schools and pupils. In 1878, of high, middle, and primary schools there were altogether 27,600, with 68,000 teachers and 2,319,000 pupils.[1] The following table shows the comparative history of educational institutions within three years, 1878–1880 (inclusive):

Year.	Institutions.	Teachers.		Pupils.	
		Male.	Female.	Male.	Female.
1878	27,672	66,309	2,374	1,715,425	610,214
1879	29,362	71,757	2,803	1,771,641	608,205
1880	30,799	74,747	2,923	1,844,564	605,781

Furthermore, hundreds of students went abroad yearly, and returning, powerfully influenced the destiny of their country.

---

[1] Count Okuma's pamphlet.

III.—NEWSPAPERS.

It was in 1869 that the Emperor sanctioned the publication of newspapers. Magazines, journals, periodicals and newspapers sprung up in a night. The number of newspapers published in 1882 was about 113, and of miscellaneous publications about 133. It is to be noted that the newspapers defied the old censorship of prohibition under very sanguinary pains and penalties. Their circulation increased every year. The total newspaper circulation in 1874 was but 8,470,269, while in 1877 it was 33,449,529. In his consular report of 1882, Consul-General Van Buren makes an approximate estimate of the annual aggregate circulation of a dozen noted papers of Tokio to be not less than 29,000,000 copies.[1]

The publication of books and translations kept pace with the growth of newspapers. Observing the effects of these literary activities, Mr. Griffis well says: " It is the writer's firm belief, after nearly four years of life in Japan, mingling among the progressive men of the empire, that the reading and study of books printed in the Japanese language have done more to transform the Japanese mind and to develop an impulse in the direction of modern civilization than any other cause or series of causes."

Meanwhile, great changes were affecting law and religion. Here it is sufficient to observe that the old law which had been hitherto altogether arbitrary—either the will of the Emperor or of the Shogun—was revised on the model of the Napoleonic code and soon published throughout the land. The use of torture to obtain testimony was wholly and forever abolished.

With the incoming of Western science and Christianity, old faiths began to lose their hold upon the people. The new religion spread yearly. Missionary schools were instituted in several parts of the country. Christian churches were

[1] Consular Report of the U. S., No. 25, p. 182.

built in almost all of the large cities and towns, and their number increased constantly. Missionaries and Christian schools had no inconsiderable influence in changing the ideas of the people.

Such, in brief, have been the changes in the industrial, social and religious condition of Japan from 1868 to 1881. After this study we shall not much wonder at the remarkable political change of Japan during the same period, which I shall endeavor to describe in the next chapter.

CHAPTER V.

PROGRESS OF THE CONSTITUTIONAL MOVEMENT FROM THE ABOLITION OF FEUDALISM TO THE PROCLAMATION OF OCTOBER 12, 1881.

The leaders of the Restoration were of an entirely different type from the court nobles of former days. They were, with a few exceptions, men of humble origin. They had raised themselves from obscurity to the highest places of the state by sheer force of native ability. They had studied much and travelled far. Their experiences were diverse; they had seen almost every phase of society. If they were now drinking the cup of glory, most of them had also tasted the bitterness of exile, imprisonment, and fear of death. Patriotic, sagacious, and daring, they combined the rare qualities of magnanimity and urbanity. If they looked with indifference upon private morality, they were keenly sensitive to the feeling of honor and to public morals. If they made mistakes and did not escape the charge of inconsistency in their policy, these venial faults were, for the most part, due to the rapidly changing conditions of the country. No other set of statesmen of Japan or of any other country, ancient or modern, have witnessed within their lifetime so many social and political transformations. They saw the days when feudalism flourished —the grandeur of its rulers, its antique chivalry, its stately etiquette, its ceremonial costumes, its codes of honor, its rigid social order, formal politeness, and measured courtesies. They also saw the days when all these were swept away and replaced by the simplicity and stir of modern life. They accordingly "have had to cast away every tradition, every habit, and every principle and mode of action with which even the youngest of them had to begin official life."

The ranks of this noble body of statesmen and reformers are now, alas! gradually breaking. Saigo, the elder, is no more. Kido and Iwakura have been borne to their graves. Okubo and Mori have fallen under the sword of fanatics. But, thanks to God, many of them yet remain and bear the burdens of the day.

I have mentioned in Chapter III. the overthrow of feudalism and its causes. Its immediate effect on the nation, in unifying their thoughts, customs, and habits, was most remarkable. From this time we see the marked growth of common sentiment, common manners, common interest among the people, together with a love of peace and order.

While the government at home was thus tearing down the old framework of state, the Iwakura Embassy in foreign lands was gathering materials for the new. This was significant, inasmuch as five of the best statesmen of the time, with their staff of forty-four able men, came into association for over a year with western peoples, and beheld in operation their social, political and religious institutions. These men became fully convinced that " the wealth, the power, and the happiness of a people," as President Grant told them, " are advanced by the encouragement of trade and commercial intercourse with other powers, by the elevation and dignity of labor, by the practical adaptation of science to the manufactures and the arts, by increased facilities of frequent and rapid communication between different parts of the country, by the encouragement of immigration, which brings with it the varied habits and diverse genius and industry of other lands, by a free press, by freedom of thought and of conscience, and a liberal toleration in matters of religion."[1]

The impressions and opinions of these men on the importance of a free and liberal policy can be gleaned from the speeches they made during the western tour, and some of their writings and utterances on other occasions.

The chief ambassador, Iwakura, in reply to a toast made to him in England, said: " Having now become more intimately acquainted with her (England's) many institutions, we

---

[1] C. Lanman, The Japanese in America, p. 33.

have discovered that their success is due to the *liberal* and energetic spirit by which they are animated."[1]

Count Ito, the present President of the Privy Council, in his speech at San Francisco, said: " While held in absolute obedience by despotic sovereigns through many thousand years, our people knew no freedom or liberty of thought. With our material improvement they learned to understand their rightful privileges, which for ages have been denied them."[2]

Count Inouye, the ex-Minister of State for Agriculture and Commerce, in his memorial to the government in 1873, said: "The people of European and American countries are for the most part rich in intelligence and knowledge, and they preserve the spirit of independence. And owing to the nature of their polity they share in the counsels of their government. Government and people thus mutually aid and support each other, as hand and foot protect the head and eye. The merits of each question that arises are distinctly comprehended by the nation at home, and the government is merely its outward representative. But our people are different. Accustomed for ages to despotic rule, they have remained content with their prejudices and ignorance. Their knowledge and intelligence are undeveloped and their spirit is feeble. In every movement of their being they submit to the will of the government, and have not the shadow of an idea of what 'a right' is. If the government makes an order, the whole country obeys it as one man. If the government takes a certain view, the whole nation adopts it unanimously. . . . The people must be recalled to life, and the Empire be made to comprehend with clearness that the objects which the government has in view are widely different from those of former times."[3]

---

[1] Mossman's New Japan, p. 442.

[2] C. Lanman, The Japanese in America, p. 14.

[3] The translation of the whole memorial is given in C. Lanman's Leading Men of Japan, p. 87.

If the passages quoted illustrate statesmen's zeal to introduce western civilization, and to educate the people gradually
to political freedom and privileges, their actions speak more
eloquently than their words. In order to crush that social
evil, the class system, which for ages had been a curse, the
government declared all classes of men equal before the law,
delivered the *eta*—the class of outcasts—from its position of
contempt, abolished the marriage limitations existing between
different classes of society, prohibited the wearing of swords,
which was the peculiar privilege of the nobles and the
Samurai; while to facilitate means of communication and to
open the eyes of the people to the wonders of mechanical art,
they incessantly applied themselves to the construction of rail-
roads, docks, lighthouses, mining, iron, and copper factories,
and to the establishment of telegraphic and postal systems.
They also codified the laws, abolished the use of torture in
obtaining testimony, revoked the edict against Christianity,
sanctioned the publication of newspapers, established by the
decree of 1875 the "Genro-in (a kind of Senate) to enact laws
for the Empire, and the Daishin-in to consolidate the judicial
authority of the courts,"[1] and called an assembly of the
prefects, which, however, held but one session in Tokio.

While the current of thought among the official circles was
thus flowing, there was also a stream, in the lower region of
the social life, soon to swell into a mighty river. Social
inequality, that barrier which prevents the flow of popular
feeling, being already levelled, merchants, agriculturists,
tradesmen, artisans and laborers were now set at liberty to
assert their rights and to use their talents. They were no
longer debarred from places of high honor.

The great colleges and schools, both public and private,
which were hitherto established and carried on exclusively
for the benefit of the nobles and the Samurai, were now open
to all. And in this democracy of letters, where there is no
rank or honor but that of talent and industry, a sentiment

---

[1] The Imperial decree of 1875.

was fast growing that the son of a Daimio is not necessarily wiser than the son of a peasant.

Teachers of these institutions were not slow to infuse the spirit of independence and liberty into their pupils and to instruct the people in their natural and political rights. Mr. Fukuzawa, a schoolmaster, an author, and a lecturer, the man who exercised an immense influence in shaping the mind of young Japan, gave a deathblow to the old ideas of despotic government, and of the blind obedience of the people, when he declared that *government exists for the people and not the people for the government,* that the government officials are the servants of the people, and the people their employer. He also struck a heavy blow at the arrogance and extreme love of military glory of the Samurai class, with whom to die for the cause of his sovereign, whatever that cause might be, was the highest act of patriotism, by advocating that " Death is a democrat, and that the Samurai who died fighting for his country, and the servant who was slain while caught stealing from his master, were alike dead and useless."

In a letter to one of his disciples, Mr. Fukuzawa said : " The liberty of which I have spoken is of such great importance that everything should be done to secure its blessings in the family and in the nation, without any respect to persons. When every individual, every family and every province shall obtain this liberty, then, and not till then, can we expect to witness the true independence of the nation ; then the military, the farming, the mechanical, and mercantile classes will not live in hostility to each other ; then peace will reign throughout the land, and all men will be respected according to their conduct and real character." [1]

The extent of the influence exercised with pen and tongue by these teachers upon the nation showed that the reign of sword and brutal force was over and the day of peace and reason had dawned. The press has at last become a power.

---

[1] The translation given in C. Lanman, Leading Men of Japan, p. 47.

The increase during that period of publications, both original and translations, and of newspapers, both in their number and circulation, is marvellous. To give an illustration, the number of newspapers transmitted in the mails increased from 514,610 in the year 1873 to 2,629,648 in the year 1874 —an increase of 411 per cent in one year—"a fact which speaks volumes for the progress of civilization."[1]

These newspapers were soon to become the organs of political parties which were in the process of formation. The most prominent among these political societies was the *Ri-shi-sha*, which finally developed into the present Liberal party. At the head of this party was Count Itagaki, a man of noble character and of marked ability, who had rendered many useful services to the country in the time of the Restoration and had for some years been a member of the cabinet, but who in 1875 resigned his office and became "the man of the people." He and his party contributed greatly to the development of constitutional ideas. Whatever may be said as to the extreme radicalism and childish freaks of the rude elements of this party, the presence of its sober members, who sincerely longed to see the adoption of a constitutional form of government and used only proper and peaceful means for the furtherance of their aim, and boldly and frankly told what they deemed the defects of the government; the presence of such a party in the country, whose masses knew nothing but slavish obedience to every act of the government, was certainly a source of great benefit to the nation at large.

In 1873, Count Itagaki with his friends had sent in a memorial to the government praying for the establishment of a representative assembly, but they had not been heeded by the government. In July, 1877, Count Itagaki with his Ri-shi-sha again addressed a memorial to the Emperor, "praying for a change in the form of government, and setting forth the reasons which, in the opinion of the members of the society, rendered such a change necessary."

[1] See the Appendix of Griffis' The Mikado's Empire.

These reasons were nine in number and were developed at great length. Eight of them formed a direct impeachment of the present government, and the ninth was a reminder that the solemn promise of 1868 had never been fulfilled. "Nothing," they conclude, "could more tend to the well-being of the country than for your Majesty to put an end to all despotic and oppressive measures, and to consult public opinion in the conduct of the government. To this end a representative assembly should be established, so that the government may become constitutional in form. The people would then become more interested and zealous in looking after the affairs of the country; public opinion would find expression, and despotism and confusion cease. The nation would advance in civilization; wealth would accumulate in the country; troubles from within and contempt from without would cease, and the happiness of your Imperial Majesty and of your Majesty's subjects would be secured."

But again the government heeded not, its attention at the time being fully occupied with the suppression of the Satsuma Rebellion. The civil war being ended, in 1878, the year which marked a decade from the establishment of the new régime, the government, persuaded that the time for popular institutions was fast approaching, not alone through representations of the Tosa memorialists, but through many other signs of the times, decided to take a step in the direction of establishing a national assembly. But the government acted cautiously. Thinking that to bring together hundreds of members unaccustomed to parliamentary debate and its excitement, and to allow them a hand in the administration of affairs of the state, might be attended with serious dangers, as a preparation for the national assembly the government established first local assemblies. Certainly this was a wise course.

These local assemblies have not only been good training schools for popular government, but also proved reasonably successful. They hold their sessions every year, in the month of March, in their respective electoral districts, and there discuss all questions of local taxation. They may also petition the central government on other matters of local interest. The members must be males of the full age of twenty-five years, who have been resident for three years in the district and pay the sum of $10 as a land tax within their district. The qualifications for electors (males only) are: an age of twenty years, registration, and payment of a land tax of $5. Voting is by ballot, but the names of the voters are to be written by themselves on the voting papers. There are now 2172 members who sit in these local assemblies, and it was from the more experienced members of these assemblies that the majority of the members of the House of Representatives of the Imperial Diet, convened for the first time last year, were chosen.

The gulf between absolute government and popular government was thus widened more and more by the institution of local government. The popular tide raised by these local assemblies was swelling in volume year by year. New waves were set in motion by the younger generation of thinkers. Toward the close of the year 1881 the flood rose so high that the government thought it wise not to resist longer. His Imperial Majesty hearing the petitions of the people, graciously confirmed and expanded his promise of 1868 by the famous proclamation of October 12, 1881:

"We have long had it in view to gradually establish a constitutional form of government. . . . . It was with this object in view that in the eighth year of Meiji (1875) we established the Senate, and in the eleventh year of Meiji (1878) authorized the formation of local assemblies. . . . . We therefore hereby declare that we shall, in the twenty-third year of Meiji (1890) establish a parliament, in order to carry into full effect the determination we have announced; and we charge our faithful subjects bearing our commissions to make, in the meantime, all necessary preparations to that end."

www.ingramcontent.com/pod-product-compliance
Lightning Source LLC
Chambersburg PA
CBHW031804090426
42739CB00008B/1150

9 7 8 3 3 3 7 1 6 5 6 2 8